BOOK 2

Lift Off on Financial Investing

Lift Off Strategy for Insurance

Lift Off Strategy for Investments

Lift Off Strategy for Taxes

© *by Royal Tech Writers & Translators*

AF719873

While every precaution has been taken in the preparation of this book, the publisher assumes no responsibility for errors or omissions, or for damages resulting from the use of the information contained herein.

LIFT OFF WITH FINANCIAL INVESTMENTS

First edition. September 7, 2023.

Copyright © 2023 Sharon O'Maley.

ISBN: 979-8223564270

Written by Sharon O'Maley.

Royal Tech Writers & Translators and the editors who have been involved with the production of this manual have produced this book as an educational tool for individuals or professionals in the most accurate and current manner possible. It is not written, however, for the purpose of giving legal advice to the reader or sold to render legal, accounting or any other professional service.

Information may change over a period of time so RTW&T disclaim responsibility for any omission or inaccuracies in this particular text. RTW&T, consequently, does not accept liability for any actual or perceived loss resulting from the information in this book.

Page

Chapter 1

Lift Off Strategy for Insurance

Financial Planning with HMO

A Health Maintenance Organization (HMO) is any health-care delivery system that offers both coverage for medical care and the care itself for a prearranged price. When a person joins one, either as an individual member or through company, the employee or his employer pays a monthly sum to the plan he has chosen. The HMO then assumes responsibility for the medical expenses of that individual as long as he uses the providers and services it designates.

HMOs may be tightly managed group practice plans or loosely organized associations of physicians practicing in their own offices. They may be independent organizations or they may be sponsored by commercial insurance companies like CIGNA or Prudential, by Blue Cross, by hospitals, by physicians' associations, or by unions, employers, or consumers.

Nationally, HMOs enroll close to 20% of employees who have group health plans, and they are offered to more than 50% of the work force that receives health insurance from employers. Yet, despite the widespread availability of HMOs, many people remain confused about how they operate and the quality of care they provide.

Health Maintenance Organizations are the dominant model in managed care. They help to control costs by providing a full range of health services for a pre-set fee. They are supposed to cut expenses by reducing waste. But for the most part, they have not consistently performed better than indemnity insurance plans in terms of price increases. The original HMO legislation allowed the plans to peg their prices to conventional insurance premiums. Many HMOs have engaged in so-called shadow pricing to maximize their profits.

They start out offering lower prices, then raise them each year by the same percentages as the high-cost indemnity plans. They have tried to stay just a little cheaper; so that they would attract new business. As more patients signed up and larger chains began to develop, the competition grew, and some HMOs would cut their premiums by as much as 50% when a competitor moved into town.

By practicing prepaid medicine, HMOs are able to set an annual budget and then require their staff doctors to stay within it. This sometimes leads to juggling decisions about how to care for the plan's patients and managing the costs. Even so, some HMO doctors are giving better care than some higher-priced fee-for-service doctors.

For example, HMO doctors control access to specialists and surgery. Thousands of patients die every year during unnecessary operations. A doctor who prevents an unnecessary operation may be saving the patient's life. The best-managed health plans are beginning to prove that sometimes quality actually costs less. Price does not equal quality.

Financial Planning with Preferred Provider Organizations (PPO)

In between the free choice offered by an indemnity policy and the restricted choice characteristic of a health maintenance organization lies an alternative: a plan that allows one unrestricted access to any licensed physician or accredited hospital while rewarding him financially for choosing from its approved list of physicians and hospitals. Preferred providers—physicians and other caregivers, pharmacies, hospitals, laboratories, and other medical services—may be selected because they provide care at a discount to plan members or because they have developed a cost-efficient style of medical care.

The PPO approach grew out of the needs of various groups; employers experiencing large increases in health care costs and insurance companies, hospitals, and physicians who were losing business to HMOs. Employers wanted to preserve choice and control costs. Insurance companies, hospitals, and physicians wanted to retain patients in a newly competitive health care market.

Defining PPOs

The phrase "preferred provider insurance" designates the whole plan—from the perspective of the consumer. One will see the letters "PPO" (Preferred Provider Organization) or sometimes "PPA" (Preferred Provider Association) used loosely to designate the same concept. These two acronyms actually refer to the providers and institutions on the approved list, who may have created a formal organization to represent their interests or may simply have signed a contract with a sponsoring organization such as an insurance company, a hospital, or an employer. Sometimes sponsoring organizations combine in a joint venture.

Preferred provider organizations are newer to the HMO scene than Independent Practice Associations (IPA), but they were developed to compete in that market in response to the same needs. IPAs were structured to meet the needs of doctors as well as patients. PPOs took the priorities one step further to include the needs of the insuring party as well.

Advantages of PPOs

Both employers and employees find advantages in preferred provider insurance plans. Employers like the fact that these plans allow them to offer their employees better coverage at the same, or lower, cost. For example, General Hospital may agree to give a 20% discount on its services to a large employer. Now the employer can afford to offer an insurance plan that covers care at General Hospital in full. Employees like preferred provider insurance because they retain full control to choose services and providers.

Basically, a PPO is an arrangement between health care providers and employers. Doctors and other providers agree to become "preferred" providers by offering lower-than-usual rates under a contract with the employer. Employees are informed that providers are "preferred" (this also acts as a marketing tool for the providers), and have an incentive to use those providers instead of others because they have a lower deductible and coinsurance or because the deductible and coinsurance are waived entirely when the patient consults a preferred provider instead of someone outside the net-work.

Insurance in a Financial Planning Role

Life insurance can be uniquely used in financial planning. Financial planning means an individual takes a multi-period approach to savings and consumption. It implies a design to maximize the utility of lifetime income by spreading consumption in a planned way.

The principal economic purpose of life insurance is to accumulate capital. Although most commentators stress that life insurance should not be viewed principally as an investment, many other individuals and professionals feel differently. Life insurance is, in fact a superb "investment' vehicle. All conventional investment vehicles serve the same purpose, but the unique feature of life insurance is that it assures a desired accumulation at a specific, but uncertain, time, namely at the time of the insured's death. No other investment makes such a guarantee.

PPO Administration

PPOs can be organized and sponsored by a hospital, a group of doctors, a group of employees, a broker, or any combination of those. Conventional insurers are also involved in PPOs.

PPOs specialize in sophisticated data analysis, so they can find out that doctors exceed the statistical average rate of performing surgery or medical tests. The network usually calls in the high-utilization doctor and explains to him or her that utilization should be reduced (or the reason for the high rate explained); in extreme cases doctors can be told to leave the network if they don't bring their utilization rates back down.

A typical PPO pays 90% of covered expenses, and there is no deductible if one use only preferred providers, except for hospital emergency room visits, that are subject to a deductible. If one does not use providers from the plan's preferred list, he must pay a much higher deductible, and the plan will then cover only 70% of his costs above the deductible. There is no coverage for preventive and wellness care. Members are charged $3 for each prescription at specified pharmacies. The plan has a stop-loss of $3,000. The employer pays the entire premium for the employee's coverage, but the employee is required to pay a certain amount a month toward the premium cost if when covering a family.

Strategy with Disability Income Insurance

One out of every four regularly employed workers in America can expect to become disabled for a period of at least a year before reaching age 65; three and one-half million workers and their families currently draw Social Security disability benefits. Many injuries and illnesses are obviously disabling. There are others, however, such as chronic illnesses that become acute with age, or residual conditions that deteriorate over time, that become disabling even though they weren't initially too severe. For example, an older worker may have had injury years before, or an illness that had been dormant, under control or merely "livable," but that has become aggravated through the years to the point where work is extremely difficult or impossible. In such cases, an older worker may become eligible for disability benefits although the original illness or injury was not disabling.

Mechanics of Disability Income Insurance

Disability insurance is really "income replacement" insurance. It provides the disabled with a good portion of the cash he and his family need to live on during a period of disability. Compared with all other insurance policies, disability insurance is something one most certainly should not be without, particularly if he is the family breadwinner and the family depends on his income. Disability insurance differs in one major way from health insurance. Health insurance pays for hospital and doctors costs incurred as the result of an injury or accident. Disability provides the insured with money. This money replaces a large portion of income lost as the result of disability from an injury or accident. It does not pay hospital or doctor bills.

It is possible to get disability insurance that replaces 100% of one's lost income for as long as he is disabled. But coverage like that would be very expensive. It is not necessary that all of one's former income be replaced. The disabled person will not have business-related expenses such as travel and clothes. While he is on disability, he is not drawing a salary; so will be paying much less in taxes, or no taxes at all.

The money that he receives from disability insurance, if he paid the premiums himself, is tax-free. With expenses considerably less, insurance experts say that one can maintain his current lifestyle with about 60% of his income at the time he became disabled. Disability policies replace an agreed upon portion of one's income during a period of disability.

Being created to fill the gap caused when companies cease to offer guaranteed renewable and non-cancelable contracts are disability income policies that are guaranteed renewable but not non-cancelable, meaning that the company can increase the premium later on, if necessary. That privilege allows the company to charge a little less at the beginning to take into account increases in the future.

Integration

Integration is when an insurance company offers economical premiums because they mandate that disability benefits from other sources, such as social security, will reduce the benefit the company has to pay. If integration was not used and the policy holder were disabled while working and driving a car, there are a variety of places that would owe disability benefits to the individual such as social security, worker's compensation, state compensation, group disability, and individually owned disability insurance.

If each had to pay 100% of what was owed under each plan, the individual could find himself or herself being paid more to be disabled than to be working. As a result, there would be no economic incentive for a disabled worker to go back to work. This would be an undesirable situation for workers and taxpayers at large; they would be the ones who would end up paying for excessive benefits. Integration allows the systems of reimbursement to work together to make sure that adequate—but not excessive—benefits are paid.

This helps keep down the cost of insurance. Prior to the days of integration people could collect medical reimbursement from more than one source so being sick could actually be profitable. Integration came to medical insurance in order to eliminate that costly practice.

Redesigning a Policy

An example of someone redesigning a policy to reduce cost follows. A 40-year-old was offered a $3,000 per month lifetime benefit policy with a 60-day waiting period, cost-of-living increase rider, residual benefits, and option to buy more insurance for a total cost of $2,273 per year, that was almost 4% of his annual income. To reduce costs, the agent requoted the policy with benefits of $3,000 per month to age 65, a 180-day waiting period, and elimination of all the riders. The cost came to $788 per year, a little over 1% of his annual income. The lower cost policy was double, so he now has a core benefit policy that he can build on with employer or association group contracts.

Types of Disability Income Insurance

Mortgage Disability Insurance

While an individual needs a disability policy to cover a loss of income, he or she does not need someone that is specifically tied to a mortgage. Instead, one should be looking for a solid disability policy that will meet all of one's financial needs during the length of time that an individual is disabled. When one evaluates insurance needs, he or she should be concerned with all of the financial obligations that the family will be saddled with in the event of one's death, not just a mortgage. Similarly, when an individual is looking for a policy to replace a monthly income in case this individual is disabled, the monthly mortgage payment is just one factor to consider in determining how much insurance to buy.

Now the mortgage payment may be the most significant but there will be a great many other expenses also. Having a disability policy that only takes care of the monthly mortgage payment is a start, but it is certainly not enough to cover the entire monthly to cover all of the expenses one has.

A comprehensive disability policy that replaces 60% of one's monthly income is much superior to mortgage disability insurance. When an individual is buying disability policy to protect the income one that is needed to pay a mortgage or other debts, it is a good idea to keep in mind what kind of mortgage one has. With a fixed-rate mortgage, this individual knows precisely what the monthly obligation will be.

Association Disability Insurance

When an individual is a member of an organization or an association, they may offer group disability income benefits to its membership. Some of the plans are enticing because of their low cost, but the plans may be inadequate. They may have impossible-to-meet definitions of disability. The policyholder would not be considered disabled even if the only remaining means of self-support were selling pencils on the street corner. These are some limitations to Association Disability Insurance:

- Contracts can be canceled by insurance company or association.
- Rates typically increase as one gets older or benefits are reduced as he or she gets older.
- Insurance company can increase rates.
- Restrictive definitions of disability.
- No, or limited, coverage for partial losses.
- Limited or no protection ensuring future insurability.
- Limited benefits for mental, nervous, and emotional disorders.
- Integration with other sources of compensation; that is if other sources like an employer plan or Social Security pay, the association plan reduces or eliminates the payment of benefits.

The policyholder has no control over what happens with an association plan. If the insurance provider decides to terminate the plan, the policyholder may find himself or herself trying to replace the benefits at what could be an inopportune time. The policyholder may be disabled or in ill health—in that case no other carrier will insure this individual and he or she will not be able to replace the benefits.

Group Disability Coverage

Disability is more likely to strike during a working career than death itself. And yet, the vast majority of workers own life insurance and not disability insurance. The fault may lie with the insurance company because they have not educated the public on the need for disability coverage. The majority of Americans need disability income insurance coverage every bit as much as the higher earners. Many of them provide it as a fringe benefit for their employees in the form of group disability insurance. Because Disability Income Insurance replaces wages lost due to sickness or a disabling injury, the employer is a logical place to look for the coverage.

Purpose of Life Insurance in Financial Planning

Life insurance offers a way to replace the loss of income that occurs when someone dies. This person is usually the person who produces the majority of income in a family situation. It is a contract between an individual as the insured person and the company or "carrier" that is providing the insurance. If the insured dies while the contract is in force, the insurance company pays a specified sum of money free of income tax – "cash benefits" – to the person or persons named as beneficiaries.

However, a good life insurance program does more than just replace the loss of income that occurs if the insured dies. It should also provide money to cover the new costs that arise after the insured's death such as funeral expenses, taxes, probate cost, the need for housekeepers and childcare, and so on. An individual may consider insuring the life of a spouse who is not earning money. That is because the spouse may be helping with the family expenses by caring for children instead of putting them in childcare. And these cash benefits should provide for the family's future needs as well, including college education for the children of the insured and part or all of the insured's spouse's retirement needs. In almost all cases, the beneficiary can use the cash benefits in the way he or she sees fit, without restriction.

Life insurance is a complex amalgamation of legal, tax, and economic elements. It can be a unique wealth creation tool that assures the accumulation of a desired amount of liquid capital at death among other things. Depending on the plan of insurance, it may also create more or less capital for lifetime needs. The next fifty years will see the largest transfer of wealth to the next generation, in history. Since we see that it is obvious the government cannot be relied on to provide for retirement, each individual must be responsible to create a successful retirement and this could depend largely on an effective estate plan to minimize taxes during one's lifetime.

Getting hurt or losing property without holding insurance is a risk one doesn't want to take. There are four basic types of insurance that one needs to consider.

- *Health Insurance*
- *Homeowner's Insurance*
- *Renter's Insurance*
- *Auto Insurance*

Let's take a closer look at each of them now.

Health Insurance

With rising medical costs, health insurance is a key type of insurance to consider. In the event of a serious accident or illness, one does not want to be uncovered. Here are a few key things about health insurance.

- *In the case that one does still qualify as a dependent on a parents' policy, some insurance plans also specify a maximum age, usually twenty-three to twenty-five years.*
- *Many employers' medical plans require a waiting period before coverage for new employees starts. So even if an individual has begun a good job with good benefits, he or she may have some period of time when he or she is not covered by any health insurance policy.*

Hospital Indemnity Plans

Basic and major medical expense plans are generally classified as indemnity contracts. These plans indemnify, or reimburse, the insured for medical expenses incurred and typically require the completion and filing of claim forms. In addition, these plans usually contain deductible and coinsurance cost sharing provisions and may restrict coverage for certain types of medical care expenditures. Indemnity plans, however, provide the insured with substantial freedom relative to the choice of physician, including whether a primary care physician or a specialist will be seen.

Hospital Indemnity plans are relatively inexpensive making them appealing to the customer. For a small amount, the policy holder can get specified benefits for each day that he or she is hospitalized. One hospital income plan costs $24.40 per month for a family and pays $60 per day up to a maximum of $24,000 when one is hospitalized for illness or injury. A spouse and children get lesser amounts per day. The maximum is higher for cancer confinement, and one gets a higher amount per day when he or she is in intensive care.

Catastrophe Major Medical

One of most the important elements of an individual's overall financial plan is protection against catastrophic medical costs. Today the cost of a serious illness or accident is often far beyond the benefits provided by the average hospitalization or major medical insurance policy. Extremely large hospital and medical bills can push expenses far over the limit basic insurance or even Medicare was ever designed to handle.

Any basic major medical or hospitalization insurance policy may be insured through right now-including Medicare-could still leave an individual with enormous bills to pay especially if he or she is confined to a nursing home for convalescent or custodial care.

Purpose of The Plan

The Catastrophe Major Medical plan protects an individual when a basic health insurance plan limits coverage against extraordinary hospital-medical-surgical-convalescent expenses. It also helps an individual when the dollar benefits paid by the health insurance are limited per year and are limited again as to what will and will not be covered

Traditional Health Insurance

The traditional health insurance is broken into three categories: Basic Medical (or Hospitalization), Major Medical, and Medical/ Surgical.

Basic Medical (Hospitalization)

Hospitalization covers the cost of a hospital stay—within limitations. The insurance company only covers a limited number of days in the hospital and will only pay an amount that they have previously determined for each day—no matter what the actual cost of a day's stay in the hospital. Probably the most well-known basic medical benefit plan is Blue Cross hospitalization. A typical hospitalization plan from Blue Cross will cover the first 120 days in the hospital each calendar year providing the policy holder uses a hospital that participates in the Blue Cross program.

Major Medical

Major medical covers specified doctors' bills not incurred during hospitalization or surgical procedures, and can be purchased separately or as a package with hospitalization. These plans generally require the policy holder to submit medical bills, which after review, are reimbursed to the policy holder.

Major medical plans typically cover a broad list of medical expenditures, including hospital expense, surgical expense, physician (non-surgical) expense, private duty nursing, diagnostic X-ray and laboratory services, prescription drug expense, artificial limbs and organs, ambulance services, and many other types of medical expenses when prescribed by a duly licensed physician.

Medical / Surgical

Medical / Surgical is really part of hospitalization coverage—the part that pertains to the actual services of the doctors involved—the surgeon, the anesthesiologist, the physical therapist, etc. IT usually also covers specified surgeries done on an outpatient basis. This type of insurance typically covers totally or in some cases partially—room and board; medical supplies; routine nursing care; use of the operating room, recovery room, etc.; doctor bills as specified in the policy; and food.

Short term medical insurance provides high-limit medical expense coverage, on an indemnity basis, for a relatively short period of time. At the time of purchase, the insured can choose a period of coverage that may be as short as thirty days, up to as long as 180 or 185 days (i.e., approximately six months). Several deductible and coinsurance options exist, with the premium cost varying according to the specific deductible and coinsurance provisions selected. Limits of coverage as high as $1 million - 2 million are typically available in the marketplace.

Homeowners Insurance

Protecting one's home has been a basic survival instinct since cave man days. But today one uses a more civilized form of protection. Instead of using spears and rocks, an individual can now protect his or her belongings with insurance. And since the "one cave fits all" approach is now extinct, homeowners' products also vary depending on the type of home in which one dwells.

If an individual is planning on buying a home, he or she needs to have an understanding of homeowner's insurance. For most people, their home is their single most valuable possession—and their biggest investment. Homeowners insurance protects an investment as well as the owner household possessions.

Most buy homeowners' insurance because it is a condition of getting and keeping a mortgage. However, homeowners insurance is much more than a requirement. It is a peace of mind, security and protection for property and possessions.

Today's homeowners insurance has many features that allows an individual to custom design a policy that is right for each individual. The traditional homeowners program offers protection for his or her home structures, personal property, as well as liability safeguards in case the policyowner is sued.

Homeowner's insurance typically has two main sections: Section I covers the property of the insured, and Section II provides personal liability coverage to the insured. Almost anyone who wants to own or lease property needs homeowner's insurance of some kind.

Section I Coverage (Property)

There should be four basic property protections for mobile homeowners. These are usually subject to a minimum deductible of $250 and increments of $250.

Coverage A: The Dwelling

This should cover the actual mobile home on the residence premises. It should also cover materials and supplies that are located on or next to the "residence premises which one uses in constructing, altering or repairing the mobile house or any attachments on the residence premise.

However, this will normally not cover the land on which the mobile house or the attachments structures sit.

Coverage B (Outbuilding or Other Unattached Structures)

Coverage B covers other structures within the residence premises but set apart from the house by clear space. This would include structures connected to the house only be a fence or utility line. These structures might include a detached garage, utility shed or a gazebo. However, it usually would not cover any structure which one uses wholly or partly for business or any structure which one has rented out, or which one could be holding out for rent.

Coverage C (Personal Property)

Coverage C refers to personal property which an individual owns or uses anywhere in the world. With a special request, items such as these can also be covered; personal property owned by others while the property is on the part of the residence property which the insured occupies or property owned by a guest or employee while the property is in any residence which the insured owns.

Coverage D (Loss of Use)

If the insured individual experiences a loss as a result of a covered peril where the mobile home becomes uninhabitable, the insurance company will normally provide the insured with either of these benefits. Additional Living expenses occurs because the insured and members of his or her household have increased expenses to maintain the normal standard of living outside the residence property. Fair Rental Value is when the insurer chooses to pay the fair rental value of that part of the mobile home where the insured resides and which has been damaged or destroyed.

Section II Coverage (Liability Protection)

There are at least two basic liability protections that an individual will want to get. Like all liability protections, it should cover one against injury to other people—and not to oneself or to members of the household. These are generally not subject to a deductible and they can include the following.

Coverage E (Personal Liability)

Coverage E gives the insured protection when a claim or a suit is brought against him or her for bodily injuries or property damage to people other than the insured or members of the insured's household.

Coverage F (Medical Payments)

Coverage F pays for medical expenses that follow an accident regardless of fault when the accident occurs within the residence premises. An incident has to have been incurred or ascertained within a three year period of the date of the accident.

Lowering Homeowner Insurance Costs

Insurance is a very competitive business and the price one pays for his or her homeowners' insurance can vary by hundreds of dollars, depending on the insurance company one buys the policy from. Companies offer several types of discounts, but they do not offer the same discount or the same amount of discount in all states. Here are some elements that the consumer will probably consider:

- ***Element of Security*** ~~ *An individual can get discounts of at least 5% for a smoke detector, burglar alarm, or dead-bolt locks. Some insurance companies give discounts on the premiums by as much as 15 or 20% if an individual installs a sophisticated sprinkler system and a fire and burglar alarm that rings at the police station or other monitoring facility.*
- ***Element of Shopping*** ~~ *After one option is presented to a consumer by an insurance agent, he or she will probably go shopping around to get advice from friends, insurance companies, state insurance department, and consumer guides. One thing*

stands however, the wise consumer wants quality even if it costs a bit more.

- ***Element of Group Purchase*** *~~ A consumer will have many advantages to purchasing both auto and home insurance policies from the same insurance company. An individual can save 5 to 15% of the premium if he or she buys two or more policies from the same insurance company.*
- ***Element of Deductible*** *~~ The consumer will probably want to lower the deductible in order to save some money. Deductibles start at about $250 and by increasing it to $500, the homeowner could save up to 12%; $1,000, up to 24%; $2,500 up to 30%; and $5,000, up to 37%.*
- ***Element of Loyalty*** *~~ If an individual keeps coverage with a company for several years, he or she may receive special reductions in their premiums. If a policyowner has had insurance with the same company for three to five years, he receives 5% reduction. If the policyowner has had insurance with the same company for six years or more, he or she receives a 10% discount.*

Renter's Insurance

Perhaps someone thinks, "I don't need to worry about insurance for my home because I'm only renting/leasing an apartment." The fact is, however, that a landlord's insurance does not cover personal property. It will only cover damage to the actual construction. Renter's insurance will cover losses and damage and can insure one in the event that someone endures an accident while on personal property.

In 1994, there were approximately 451,000 structural fires. Of these, 341,000 were in one or two-family dwellings, 97,000 were in apartments, and 13,000 were in dormitories, boarding houses, hotels, and other rental units. The property losses from these fires was $4,317,000,000. The amount lost in apartment fires was $678,000,000. Somebody obviously lost something of value. But how does one measure that value? The loss for most renters is not necessarily a room full of antiques

Another risk that a tenant may have is a clause called a subrogation clause. Under this clause the insurer can seek reimbursement from parties legally responsible for damages that the insurer has paid to the landlord. If the tenant is insured, the tenant's insurance company would have defended him against this subrogation claim and paid the damages had he been found legally responsible.

Renter's Insurance Coverage

Renter's insurance will not only cover the cost of replacing the contents, but it will also provide loss of use protection that will help one pay for temporary housing while the apartment or rental house is being repaired. This can be of significant value when one is forced to move to a local motel or hotel while the construction crews arrive to clean up and to rebuild. Most people do not think of that expense.

Renter's insurance is offered by most companies that sell homeowner's insurance and can be purchased in different levels of coverage. An individual can insure property in two different ways.

- *Actual cash value—This coverage considers the age and condition of the item at the time of the damage or loss, and pays only what it is worth to replace it with an item of similar condition.*
- *Replacement value—This pays the cost to replace the covered item with a comparable new item. Replacement value policies usually cost more, and may have restrictions.*

Tenants or renters insurance is really a form of homeowners policy. The personal property coverage could also be called content coverage since it insures the contents of the apartment. The tenant has to determine the value of the property and the renter's premium is based on this amount. So the roof, walls and the floor are the landlord's responsibility, but the possessions that an individual has collected over the years will be covered with Renters Insurance Policy.

Auto Insurance

If an individual owns a car, understanding auto insurance is a must—most states will not even issue a registration without it. Accidents happen. No matter how short a distance one has to travel, he or she needs to have protection should something go wrong.

The ownership, maintenance, or use of automobiles creates both property and liability loss exposures. The automobile loss exposures of most organizations can be insured under the business auto coverage form. In addition to the business auto coverage form, there are two coverage forms designed to meet specialized auto insurance needs.

Personal auto insurance protects the insured and his or her family when operating or riding in the automobile and any injury sustained in an auto accident. It pays for medical expenses and for lost work. Auto insurance protects the insured's financial security in the case that he or she is sued as a result of loss or injuries to other parties, following an accident when a member of the family or a friend or relative was driving after being given permission to drive by the insured or the spouse of the insured.

Most states now require proof of financial responsibility if one is involved in an accident, ticketed, or renewing a license. Most states also require owners of automobiles to carry a minimum amount of bodily injury and property damage liability insurance.

Automobile Loss Exposures

Automobile loss exposures include both property exposures and liability exposures. The property exposures have three elements.

The item subject to loss

- The item subject to loss is one or more automobiles in which the organization has a financial interest. The property loss exposures posed by ownership of mobile equipment can be insured under inland marine policies.

The cause of loss

- The mobility of autos means that they are more likely than fixed property to be damaged or destroyed by certain causes of loss. An example is the collision of automobiles with one another or with other objects. This is an exposure unique to motor vehicles. Also for the reason of self-propelling, autos are easier to steal than property of similar size and weight that does not move under its own power. But this factor can also make them less liable for other types of loss.

The financial impact of the loss

- The main consequences of damage to or destruction of an auto are decreases or losses of the auto's value, and the loss of use of the auto until it can be repaired or replaced.

Some other auto exposures could be Auto No-Fault, Uninsured Motorists, and Auto Medical Payments.

Personal Auto Insurance

The most common policy in force now is the personal auto policy. It breaks down the insurance protection into four areas:

- *liability coverage;*
- *medical payments;*
- *uninsured motorist coverage;*
- *physical damage to an auto.*

This basic policy is designed for private passenger automobiles only. If an individual drives a truck, he or she must confirm that whomever they drive it for, carries business or commercial insurance. There are two types of coverage that one can get in an auto policy. One is Liability Protection and the other is Comprehensive Protection.

While the size of the auto insurance package is primarily up to the owner to decide, most states have enacted compulsory insurance laws requiring drivers to have at least a minimum amount of auto liability insurance.

Insurance is not something to be lax about. One accident, one surgery, or even one cold can set an individual back. What's more, doctors report late or missed payments just as quickly as do credit companies

Chapter 2

Lift Off Strategy for Investments

The best thing that an individual can do to defend himself or herself where investments are concerned is to understand what he or she has. Start with learning to read a brokerage statement. If a broker hosts an annual statement reading clinic, it would be a good idea to encourage a client to attend it.

An individual's risk tolerance is the ability or willingness to endure declines in the value of investments while waiting for them to return a profit that will help meet investment goal. Some investors find it easy to ignore market fluctuations and to focus on their long-term investing goals. Others become anxious when their portfolio declines in value by even a small percentage. An individual's emotional makeup plays a significant role in how one is allocating his or her investment assets.

It is important for an investor to consider how he or she would react to a 20% or 25% decline in the value of a stock investment—a typical "bear market" occurrence. A bear market loses value over an extended period of time. Keep in mind:

- *Over the past four decades, bear markets have occurred, on average, about once every five years.*
- *In the worst of the bear markets since World War II, the Standard & Poor's® 500 Composite Stock Price Index—which tracks the stocks of 500 of the largest U.S. companies and reflects the overall*

health of the U.S. stock market—fell by −48% from January 1973 to October 1974.

Keep in mind, too, that all investments—even "super-safe" choices like bank accounts or money market funds—are subject to some type of risk. A disciplined investment approach may provide a firmer footing as investors weather the ups and downs of the market.

Following are 20 guidelines that one can use when starting to invest:

- *Only buy stock where research information is available through either research departments or other statistical services.*
- *Buy stocks only when the technical pattern confirms fundamental judgment.*
- *Sell quickly if the stock does not act as anticipated.*
- *Try not to be overly bullish or bearish.*
- *Trade with the market and not against it.*
- *Do not attempt to squeeze the last point out of a move.*
- *Expect the market to do the unexpected.*
- *Commissions are a small price to pay for capital preservation.*
- *Do not overstay trading positions, as greed is a trader's constant and greatest enemy.*
- *Reduce exposure in a market that may be in the process of "topping out" after an extended run.*
- *Learn from one's mistakes, study one's weaknesses.*
- *Do not look back as this can easily lead to distortion of current and future judgments*

Time Horizon

The time horizon is the number of years one has available to invest. It includes the time until reaching a goal—as well as the period, however long or short, when a withdrawal can be made from the investment.

For example, if an individual is saving for retirement, the time horizon should include not only the time until retirement but also the years in retirement, while living on retirement savings. At thirty years old one should anticipate an investment time frame of fifty to sixty years or more, because life expectancy is likely to be eighty years or more. And, if one plans to leave a portion of the retirement savings to heirs, the time horizon will extend well beyond the investor's life span.

Similarly, if saving for college, the time horizon should include the number of years until a child starts school, plus the years during which he or she will be enrolled. Keep in mind:

- *The longer the time until one will need the money, the more time he or she has to weather the markets' periodic swings. As a result, the longer the time horizon, the more aggressively one can consider investing.*
- *As one approaches his or her goal, a portfolio has less time to recover from market dips, so it would be a good idea to gradually shift to a more conservative asset allocation.*

Market Timing

Market timing as an investment strategy, can have significant effects on investment dollars. In recent years, rapid fluctuations and unprecedented high levels in both long term and short-term interest rates have affected all segments of our economy. Most often affected are income-oriented investors, who face the same dilemma each time they have excess funds to invest: Which way will rates go next and how long will they stay there? Is there an answer? No one really knows what direction, for any length of time, interest rates will take, until after the fact.

Some investors play the speculation game like this: "I think rates are going up. Therefore, I'll stay in short term investments so I can be liquid enough to lock up higher rates later." With equal conviction, other investors might say, "I think rates are going down. Therefore, I want to lock up these high rates now in medium to long term investments."

The Risk Vs. Return Trade-Off

Investment vehicles vary in terms of risk, from the safer money market securities to the highly volatile futures and commodity offerings. Overall, the amount of risk investors take will correspond to the return they can potentially earn. In other words, high risk generally correlates with high return, and lower risk with lower return. In general:

- *A stock investment has the potential for unlimited returns, but it is also possible to lose the entire investment—Higher risk with no guarantees*
- *Bonds pay a stated rate of interest, and one will recover the entire amount of the investment at maturity—Moderate return, fairly low risk (exceptions: non-investment grade, high-yield bonds)*
- *U.S. Treasury bonds, bills, and notes, backed by the full faith and credit of the U.S. Government—Low return, low risk*

Types of Brokers

Once an individual has decided what his or her objectives are, it is time to start looking for a registered broker-dealer. There are several places to look, including:

- *Traditional Brokers*
- *Discount Brokers*
- *Online Brokers*

Traditional Brokers

Full-service brokerage firms are a solid way to invest without extensive research or legwork. Most firms will provide clients with personalized, expert advice, newsletters filled with their research and findings, plus a wide variety of services—including accounts with credit and checking capabilities.

Discount Brokers

While the assistance could be less personalized, the transaction costs will be significantly lower with a discount broker. Discount brokerage firms do not pay their employees based on the amount of trading done by their customers, so their brokers have no incentive to encourage to trade extensively nor to opt for specific investments.

Online Brokers

The Internet has had quite an impact on the brokerage industry. More and more investors are shedding their traditional brokerage relationships and giving online investing a try. Many women enjoy online investing because of its low fees, easy access, and anonymity.

An investor has several options when it comes to selecting a firm with which to open an online brokerage account. One way to begin is with a discount brokerage firm that offers their clients high-integrity products and services at a significantly lower rate than full service firms do.

With a discount broker, an individual can invest funds in a full range of products including individual equities, bonds and other fixed income securities, mutual funds, money market accounts and more. Although many discount brokerages are able to service their clients personally, the only thing that can not be had with such a firm is direct investment advice. It is up to the investor to ultimately make his or her own investment decisions

Beginners and Online Brokers

The major difference between traditional and online brokers lies in the trafficking of information. Traditional brokers will do some homework for the investor for pay, of course. In the case of online investing, the burden is on the investor to roll up his or her sleeves and study.

Regardless of the route they take, beginning investors ought to take a step back and educate themselves before making any investment decisions. Once well informed and armed with a solid understanding of the market and the companies they're watching, even the most timid investors can make smart choices online – and that translates to profits.

Types of Investments

There are a variety of investment instruments and all of them can be utilized in a successful investment. An individual can learn a lot about investments and how and when to invest but by and large a financial planner can put you on the cutting edge of investments and how to ratio your portfolio.

Municipal Bond Investing

- Municipal bonds are debt obligations of states, local municipalities and other public authorities. The interest paid on municipal bonds is not subject to federal income taxes. When analyzing the possibility of investing in municipal bonds, an investor should consider the following in developing a strategy:

- *Review the slope of the municipal yield curve; it may be feasible to purchase long-term maturities of rates that are substantially higher.*
- *Do not "reach" for securities providing yields well in excess of those generally available in a particular market sector. There are usually negative reasons for such high yields. If security is important, avoid*

such situations.

- *Research the security provisions being pledged to determine the impact current economic trends could have upon the issue's ability to honor those provisions.*
- *Consider call provisions in purchasing municipal securities; try to lock in today's high coupons by choosing bonds with the maximum call protection.*
- *Make purchases in amounts of $25,000 face value or more, if possible. This enhances the ability to sell securities efficiently in the secondary market prior to bond maturity.*
- *Do not confine municipal purchases to only one issuer. If possible, diversify geographically and across market sectors (i.e., general obligations, public power, housing bonds, and industrial development) to protect the portfolio against adverse market conditions.*
- *Consider the total tax picture, including local income and personal property taxes. Be aware of the capital appreciation tax impact upon securities purchased at a discount.*
- *Obtain as much information as possible on the creditworthiness of the issuer. Study the prospectus if available. Disclosure of facts made in such documents is relevant to the investment security and level of risk involved and should have a bearing upon a investment decision.*
- *Request the rating levels assigned by Moody's and Standard & Poor's.*
- *Review a portfolio regularly to determine whether financial objectives are being met.*

Money Market Funds

Money Market Funds are simply co-mingled funds that invest in short term securities of a low-risk nature. Since these funds invest primarily in securities issued by the U.S. government, banking institutions and prime rate corporations, they are considered quite safe for the average investor.

The return, or yield, on money market funds has averaged between one to two points under the current prime rate. The return when compared to other investment vehicles may be equal to, above or below, depending on prevailing interest rates.

Like all managed funds, money is gathered from many different investors, and the resulting pool of cash is used to acquire particular securities. Each fund buys various government and bank notes and the details of these investments are contained in the fund's prospectus that each purchaser must receive and read prior to making an investment.

People with years of experience in this field typically manage these funds. Their experience and the fund's past performance are also spelled out in the prospectus. However, historical performance does not guarantee future performance. Some of these money market funds require an initial investment as low as $500, others require $5,000. After making the first investment, one may usually then make additional contributions of a lesser amount.

Another attractive feature of money market funds is that they are liquid. An individual may withdraw money when needed quite quickly. Some funds even provide investors with a check writing privilege that allows them to write checks on the investment. When the draft is presented for payment, an appropriate amount of the fund is liquidated. The investor's money has earned interest during this period of float. No other investment gives the individual investor this combination of safety, market sensitive earnings and liquidity.

An Insured Account

In recent years, the headlines have been all too full of bank and savings and loan failures. However, these firms had been advertising that all accounts are insured. Yet, some people are losing money. For example, one depositor spread his money around among several branch offices of the same bank, only to learn that only the first $100,000 was covered.

It is easy to understand why the public is confused about the safety of their deposits in a federally insured institution. For all the questions about Federal Deposit Insurance, there have been many suggestions and opinions.

One thing for certain is that the federal government (aided by massive transfers authorized by Congress) has developed a way to clean up the shortfall and design a plan to prevent similar problems from happening in the future. Some bank and savings institutions are still insured by state organizations and this information does not apply to them.

Insured Items

All types of deposits received by a financial institution in its usual course of business are insured. For example, savings deposits, checking deposits, deposits in NOW accounts, Christmas Club accounts and time deposits including certificates of deposit, ("CDs") are all insured deposits. Cashiers' checks, money orders, officers' checks and outstanding drafts drawn on the institution are also insured.

Certified checks, letters of credit, and travelers' checks, for which an insured depository institution is primarily liable, also are insured when issued in exchange for money or its equivalent, or for a charge against a deposit account.

Non-Insured Items

FDIC does not protect a person holding common stock, preferred stock, bonds or debentures issued by an institution. This became a major issue with the failure of one large organization where depositors had transferred low interest savings to the purchase of non-insured debentures. Deposits which are only payable overseas rather than in the United States, are not insured by the FDIC. Securities, mutual funds, annuities and similar types of investments are not covered by deposit insurance.

Treasury securities purchased by an institution on a customer's behalf, or held for safekeeping, are also not insured. The FDIC does not protect creditors (other than depositors) and shareholders of a failed bank or savings association.

Retirement Accounts

A corporate retirement plan with funds placed into an insured institution after December 19, 1992 is always insured up to $100,000 regardless of the number of plan participants. Provided that the institution met the FDIC standards as "adequately capitalized", there is "pass through" insurance for each participant up to $100,000.

The FDIC charges insured institutions a fee that varies based on the financial strength of the institution. This is much like a homeowner with a wood shingle roof paying more for fire insurance. Currently, this premium averages $2.40 per $1,000 of deposits. This represents .24 percent of the institution's earnings on the deposits - a fairly small amount.

The FDIC receives in excess of $6 billion per year in premiums and maintains a substantial cash reserve. Depositors can be assured that both the Bank Insurance Fund and the Savings Association Insurance Fund are backed by the full faith and credit of the United States.

Cash Investments

Cash investments include money-market funds - taxable and tax-free, or government, U.S. Treasury bills, and certificates of deposit (CDs). Money-market funds earn interest daily and are priced at a constant $1.00 per share. The interest rate changes daily and is low, relative to long-term bonds. U.S. Treasury bills mature in three, six, mine, or twelve months. The minimum investment is $10,000. They are bought at a discount (less than face value) and mature at par (face value). The yield is fixed when the bill is bought and is similar to yield on money-market funds.

Market price of the bill can fluctuate, although variation is minimal because of the short time to maturity. Certificates of deposit represent sums of money placed with a bank earning a guaranteed interest rate for a stated length of time. The interest is normally paid semiannually.

Common Stocks

Stocks are shares of ownership (equity in companies). Some stocks pay dividends quarterly. If one cares about current income, he or she will want to know about the dividends that stock pays, the dollar amount, the percentage compared to what one paid for the stock, how secure the dividends are, and how often they have been increased in the past. Although healthy dividends are an attractive feature, most stocks are bought for their growth potential.

The stock price is controlled by supply and demand. Many factors influence people to buy or sell, thus driving the price. One factor is earnings. Another is earnings potential, or the company's profit or potential to make a profit. A company that consistently increases its profits from increased sales is called a growth company. Normal growth companies can show an 8% to 12% growth in profit annually. Aggressive growth companies can show around a 20% growth in profit from one year to the next.

Convertible Bonds

Convertible bonds may sometimes serve as a good compromise between the safety of bonds versus the potential of equities. Convertible bonds are debentures with a twist, the right to convert the bond into a given number of shares of stock. Since these securities are affected by factors that affect both stocks and bonds, there are many things to remember when considering investing in convertible bonds.

Advantages

The first aspect of a convertible bond to review is the conversion ratio. The conversion ratio shows how many shares of each stock $1,000 in bonds can be converted.

The high yields of convertible bonds are also attractive to many investors looking for a higher level of income than most stocks can provide. There are many technology companies whose stocks pay no dividends. However, investors may diversify their portfolios and maintain income by buying convertible bonds of these same companies.

In addition, convertibles provide downside protection. No matter how far a company's stock may decline, the convertible should only decline until its yield equals the yield of a similar quality, non-convertible bond. This quality provides investors who are afraid of volatility a way of maintaining equity exposure.

Disadvantages

Unfortunately, these advantages are not gained without a cost. The yields on convertible bonds are usually a fair amount lower than non-convertible counterparts of comparable quality. Also, convertibles usually trade at a premium to the value of the stock into which the bonds may be converted. In addition, convertibles generally have a junior position to other bonds of a corporation. Investors should also be aware of the marketability of a convertible debenture. Many convertibles are thinly traded. The spread between the bid and ask prices on some issues may be measured in points instead of an eighth of a point, which is normal for most stocks.

Over The Counter Market

The over the counter (OTC) was the first marketplace for securities trading in the U.S. After all, before two dozen brokers met under a buttonwood tree in Manhattan and formally created what is now the New York Stock Exchange, they all were OTC dealers in an over-the-counter marketplace.

In addition to its informal history spanning several hundred years, over-the-counter trading in the U.S. has a more formal history dating from the 1930's. NASDAQ stands for the National Association of Securities Dealers Automated Quotations System. In U.S. trading today, the NASDAQ is the modern, automated version of the old over-the-counter market.

The NASD (National Association of Securities Dealers) is a self-regulatory organization of securities industry companies organized to regulate the over-the-counter marketplace. The NASD was established by the 1938 Maloney Act - a series of amendments to the 1934 Securities and Exchange Act. The 1938 act required a voluntary cooperative association of broker dealers to regulate themselves and their trading - while being overseen by the SEC.

Trading Procedures

The method of trading on the over-the-counter markets is different from that of the exchanges. There are no specialists trading securities on the OTC/NASDAQ markets, as is the case with the regional exchanges, the AMEX, and the NYSE. Rather, market makers survive and prosper based on their ability to compete in a free marketplace. Because their marketplace is less stringent and formalized, there are usually many market makers in each security.

Many U.S. public corporations prefer this trading method to the NYSE and the AMEX. As a result, many companies are resisting the change to leave the NASDAQ marketplace and relocate on a formal exchange. However, the debate over trading practices on the NASDAQ in recent years has caused some market makers to leave. As a result, NASDAQ market makers per security fell from past levels particularly during 1995.

On the NYSE, the average number of common stocks per specialist is approximately twenty-five - with the highest number for one specialist being over 40. On the NASDAQ the average number of market makers per security today is 10 with 7,500 securities having an average of sixteen market makers in each.

NASDAQ Trading Volume

The NYSE is the largest equity marketplace in the world, in which resides 70% of all equities listed on U.S. exchanges. However, the

NASDAQ is the second largest securities marketplace in the U.S. - and the third largest in the world. It is the second largest in the world based on dollar trading volume.

There are 7,000 domestic and foreign securities traded on the NASDAQ, double the amount on the NYSE. The annual trading volume has been a record 100 billion shares - exceeding the NYSE. A growing institutional and foreign marketplace, over half of all NASDAQ/National Market System (NMS) volume can be attributed to institutions (trades of 10,000 shares or more) with the average trade exceeding 20,000 shares. 20% of all NASDAQ institutions are foreign.

The dramatic growth of NASDAQ is partly due to the fact that it is represented by over 400,000 sales representatives and over 6,500 principal member securities organizations. Another prime reason for the expansion of the NASDAQ marketplace came as a result of the formation of the NASDAQ National Market System (NMS) which began in April 1982. Congress mandated the NMS in 1975 to increase competition and efficiency.

Planning for Investment Risks

One's risk tolerance is the ability or willingness to endure declines in the value of investments while waiting for them to return a profit that will help meet an investment goal. Some investors find it easy to ignore market fluctuations and to focus on their long-term investing goals. Others become anxious when their portfolio declines in value by even a small percentage. One's emotional makeup plays a significant role in how one allocates investment assets.

It is well to consider how to react to a 20% or 25% decline in the value of a stock investment—a typical "bear market" occurrence. Keep in mind:

- *Bear markets occur, on average, about once every five years.*

- *In the worst of the bear markets since World War II, the Standard & Poor's® 500 Composite Stock Price Index—which tracks the stocks of 500 of the largest U.S. companies and reflects the overall health of the U.S. stock market—fell by –48% from January 1973 to October 1974.*

If the possibility of such a loss would keep an individual awake at night, he or she might choose a relatively conservative asset mix. However, in doing so, there is the risk that inflation will erode a greater percentage of returns.

Good financial planning involves both understanding different types of risk and taking steps to reduce the effects of these risks. There are several types of investment risks that should be considered in any investment. These are as follows:

- *Call Risk,*
- *Capital Risk,*
- *Credit Risk,*

- *Inflationary Risk,*

Call Risk

A form of investment risk that a bond may be called, or redeemed prior to maturity, and that the investor will be unable to reinvest the principle for the same or a higher rate of return. This risk increases when interest rates are falling and it becomes more attractive for the bond issuer to call their bonds with the higher interest rates and issue new bonds with a lower interest rate. Most bonds that do have a call provision have some protection for a specified number of years.

Capital Risk

Capital Risk is a form of investment risk that the investor may lose all or part of the capital invested. The following are additional risks that an individual will want to consider.

- *Liquidity Risk*

- *Timing Risk*
- *Interest Rate Risk*
- *Legislative Risk*
- *Market Risk*
- *Selection Risk*

Credit Risk

Credit Risk is a form of investment risk that is related to bond investing. The risk of the issuer of the bond failing or its credit rating being reduced. This could involve the loss of all or part of the invested principal.

Inflationary Risk

Inflationary Risk is a form of investment risk that measures the effect of inflation on an investment. If the after-tax return on an investment is lower than the rate of inflation, the investor will have less purchasing power at the maturity of the investment.

How Dollar-Cost Averaging Reduces Risk

Whether new to investing or a sophisticated investor, an individual may want to use dollar-cost averaging, a basic strategy favored by many financial experts.

The approach takes advantage of Wall Street's only certainty: Bond and stock prices fluctuate. With dollar-cost averaging, one makes the market's natural volatility work by lowering the average price paid for shares. All one does is invest equal amounts in a security at regular intervals.

Because the amount invested remains constant, one is able to buy more shares when the price is low and fewer shares at a higher price. As a result, the average cost per share—and the amount that was paid for the shares—will always be lower than the average market price of the shares. There's no magic to it—just simple arithmetic.

Dollar-cost averaging can help to:

- ***Reduce Investment Risk*** *~ The strategy prevents from committing substantial assets at the wrong time. Suppose one has $10,000 to invest in the stock market. If this individual invests the entire amount at once, he or she risks a large loss. For example, if one had invested $10,000 at the start of 1973, it would have dwindled to $6,270 by year-end 1974—a 37% decline. It would have been two years for the investment to recover its original value.*
- ***Invest Regularly.*** *Many mutual fund companies offer an automatic program to investors at no charge. Often it's as easy as setting up regular transfers from a bank account or money market fund account. In addition to providing an investment program a measure of discipline, one will protect him/herself from personal emotions—and the natural tendency to cease investing—in a weak market.*

Dollar-cost averaging is especially appropriate for individual retirement accounts or other long-term investments—because the longer one maintains a regular investment program, the more likely he or she will be to buy shares at a wide variety of prices.

How Diversification Reduces Risk

Diversification spreads risk across numerous financial investments, reducing the impact that poor returns from any one investment are likely to have on an overall portfolio. Diversification follows a simple logic:

- *The prices of stocks, bonds, real estate, precious metals, and other investments often do not rise and fall in tandem. When one type of investment is on the rise, another may be declining.*
- *By investing in two or more types of securities, therefore, one increases the possibility that when something is doing poorly, something else will be doing well. The winner's good performance can offset the loser's disappointing returns.*
- *The end result: A portfolio's overall performance is likely to be less volatile—that is, undergo less price fluctuation—than a portfolio invested in just one security or one type of security. Put another way, a well-diversified portfolio will achieve higher returns for a given level of risk.*

Ways to Diversify

An individual can spread risk by investing in:

- *All three primary asset classes: cash investments, bonds, and stocks. Some investors further diversify by holding real estate or precious metals.*
- *Various types of investments within the primary asset classes, which perform well under differing economic conditions.*
- *Both U.S. and foreign securities.*
- *Mutual funds, rather than individual securities. Funds pool money with that of many other investors to buy an array of securities within a single asset class or even across more than one asset class.*

Diversification cannot eliminate market risk—the possibility that stock or bond prices overall will decline over short or even extended periods. Remember, too, that when diversifying a portfolio it may decline less in down markets—but it will also rise less when markets are strong.

Chapter 3

Lift Off Strategy for Taxes

Because the tax environment is constantly changing, it's important to continually reevaluate long-term planning strategies. This is particularly true of planning for retirement. For example, when tax rates were low, deferring income was not always attractive. Depending on a personal projection of future tax rates and other factors, deferral may again be very attractive for the next several years, particularly if one is subject to the highest tax rates.

Three principles should guide a long-term approach to tax and financial issues.

- **Maximize income deferral.**
- **Evaluate investments on an after-tax basis.**
- **Consider income shifting to maximize family wealth.**

Maximize Income Deferral

The high tax rates on ordinary income and the abundance of tax brackets that exist today may prompt an individual to look hard for opportunities to defer income and the associated tax liabilities. The best chances to defer significant amounts of ordinary income for the long term are generally in the area of earned income (such as salary and bonuses) and retirement accumulation plans. An individual may also have opportunities to defer tax by using qualified retirement plans and nonqualified deferred compensation plans. Maybe one doesn't expect to be in a lower tax bracket when income is received. Even so, the ability to "invest" pretax income and allow it to compound tax deferred for several years can be very attractive.

Evaluate Investments on an After-Tax Basis

The maximum tax rate on gains from property held for longer than twelve months is 20%. (There are different, more favorable rules for small business capital gains, and less favorable rules for collectibles and certain real estate.) Ordinary income is taxed at a maximum rate of 39.6%. It is likely that every individual will be in different tax brackets in different years. Except for municipal bonds, which are generally tax-exempt for federal and state purposes, most investment income will be subject to income tax at some point. For example, the interest on passbook savings accounts is taxed annually, and the appreciation in the value of a stock is taxed when the stock is sold, while dividends are taxed annually.

When one evaluates investment options, he or she should consider investment issues such as risk and asset allocation. And one should certainly consider the effect of income taxes. Generally, income taxes will decrease an investment return, although their effect will differ at various times.

Consider Income Shifting to Maximize Family Wealth

Members of a family may pay substantially different tax rates—from a low of zero percent to a high of 39.6%. These differences in tax brackets may encourage one to shift income and assets from high-bracket individuals to low-bracket individuals, who may include children and grandchildren, as well as parents. Unmarried individuals who are at least age fourteen are subject to a 15% tax rate on income up to $25,750. Children under age fourteen are generally taxed on their investment income at the same rates as their parents, excluding the first $700, which is not taxed, and the second $700, which is taxed at 15%. Trusts that accumulate income may also offer planning opportunities

Tax Shelter Considerations

Tax sheltered and other tax-advantaged investments may provide an investor with immediate tax deductions that are "paper losses." However, a tax shelter should also be a sound investment. If the shelter does not make good economic sense before consideration is given to the tax advantages, the investment may be determined to be an "abusive shelter" and the overall investment may not be the suitable place for the investor's money in addition to the tax losses being denied.

In addition to reviewing the economics of a tax shelter investment, there are other areas to scrutinize when making an evaluation. Changes in the tax laws, specifically the "at risk rules" the "Passive Loss Limitation" and recent IRS enforcement activities, have altered the way many investors view shelters.

A balance between tax deductions and future cash flow commensurate with the risk is more important in the selection and evaluation of investments than ever before. Most sheltered investments are made in the form of limited partnerships. Each partnership has certain elements that need to be evaluated and a judgment made before reviewing the attributes of the specific investment. These elements include:

THE GENERAL PARTNER

Most partnerships are small businesses, effectively under the complete control of the general partner. An inept general partner can destroy an otherwise sound economic venture. The factors to review:

- Reputation of the general partner.
- Financial condition of the general partner.
- Are management fees reasonable?
- Are there conflicts of interest?
- How have their other programs performed?

THE LEGAL OPINION

Offerings usually include a lengthy opinion of counsel. This opinion should be read carefully. The lawyer writing the opinion must inquire into all relevant tax areas. Factors to review:

- Reputation of the firm doing the opinion.

- Tax status of investment - partnership not corporation.
- Are there disclaimers of facts? There should be none.
- Strong position as to eligibility of the tax benefits?

ECONOMICS AND CASH FLOW

Projections are usually prepared for ventures in which cash flow is reasonably predictable. Since tax shelters run the risk that tax savings may not materialize, the economics of the investment must be analyzed. Factors to review:

- Minimum tax, at risk provisions and rate of return.
- How are profits and losses allocated?
- Possibility of an over valuation of the property?
- Are cash distributions timely?
- Can there be additional assessments?
- How long is the pay back or return of investment period?
- Are the uses of invested funds understandable?
- Are there unsupported projections?
- Are the projection assumptions reasonable and supported?

Let's look at other important considerations in evaluating shelters.

Alternative Minimum Tax

When investing in shelters, the Alternative Minimum Tax can be triggered in a number of ways. In this regard, there is a maximum effective shelter point at which marginal tax rate drops. A problem can develop when an executive exercises company incentive stock options and makes use of large loans to carry the security position. This creates limited interest deductions (an excess itemized deduction) as well as a tax reference on the spread (difference between grant price and market value) that when added to other tax preferences may trigger the Alternative Minimum Tax.

The Alternative Minimum Tax is also designed to tax the passive loss incurred that is otherwise a limited tax deduction. The Alternative

Minimum Tax is paid regardless of how much additional shelter is used. Since the Alternative Minimum Tax has a rate of 6%, the most tax savings that can result per dollar of additional tax shelter is only 26 cents.

Even if regular tax exceeds the Alternative Minimum Tax, one needs to be careful about investing in shelters that benefit from the Investment Tax Credit. If the regular tax amount is reduced by the credit, the Alternative Minimum Tax may then be higher. Investment tax credits cannot be used to reduce the alternative minimum tax liability.

At Risk Provisions/Passive Loss Limitation

The deductibility of tax shelter losses is limited through enactment of the "at risk" rules and passive loss limitations. Under the provisions, tax losses from all activities other than real estate are limited to the investor's actual economic investment; the amount that may be lost is "at risk." Under real estate, deductible passive losses are limited to the passive income.

The "at risk" rules are extended to the Investment Tax Credit. These rules limit the Investment Tax Credit on both new and used property and apply to all activities other than real estate. The new provision requires a separate "at risk" computation and has its own special rules which distinguish it from the "at risk" rules applicable to tax losses. TRA '86 introduced a phase out of ITC for most investments and restricts ITC to two special classes of real estate.

The taxpayer's basis in the property is limited to their amount at risk as of the close of the taxable year. For example, if a computer costing $1 million is purchased by an individual with $200,000 in cash and an $800,000 nonrecourse note (the client is not liable for personal repayment), the taxpayer's qualified investment credit basis should be limited to the $200,000 at risk so that on the taxpayer's tax return the investment tax credit should only be $20,000 (10% of $200,000).

Under the Passive Loss ruling, losses can only offset income generated by the passive investment, as well as other passive income. If a passive real estate investment is disposed of and a gain is realized, then any remaining suspended loss may be used to offset the taxable gain realized.

For those real estate investments in which the taxpayer is materially involved and owns 10% or more of the property, the passive loss limitation rules allow for a $25,000 ceiling after expenses have offset the taxable income generated by the investment. Under this ruling, an individual's adjusted gross income determines how much of the $25,000 may be used to offset other taxable income. Once the AGI reaches $150,000 or more, the $25,000 allowance is eliminated.

Tax Strategies for Tips for High-Income, High-Net-Worth Individuals

Contribute directors' fees to retirement accounts. Earning compensation for serving on a company's board of directors may enable one to make a contribution to a tax-deferred self-employed retirement account and receive a current income tax deduction for the amount contributed. It may be possible to do this even if one is also an employee of the company, if the compensation is sufficiently segregated from a wage income***Make gifts to grandchildren or children to encourage contributions to individual retirement accounts.*** Children and grandchildren with earned income can contribute up to $2,000 (and an additional $2,000 for a spouse) annually to a tax-deferred IRA. To encourage the child or grandchild to make the maximum contribution to a tax-deferred IRA, one may make a gift to the child or grandchild that is at least equal to the after-tax cost of the IRA contribution.

Make pretax gifts to low-income parents and grandparents. Individuals in a 40% income tax bracket need income in excess of $16,666 to make a $10,000 gift to their parents or grandparents. If income could be shifted to the relative in need (for example, through the use of a trust), significantly less income would be required to fund the $10,000 gift after taxes. The ultimate savings will depend upon the relative's current income tax picture (including such factors as the relative's income tax bracket, and whether deductions and exemptions are being wasted).***Take advantage of transportation tax breaks.*** If an employer allows pre-tax salary dollars to be used for parking, mass transit, or van pooling, take advantage of the current tax savings, but be mindful of the effect on retirement benefit calculations that may result from a salary reduction.

Select the right beneficiaries for qualified retirement plans. One can maximize the time over which a retirement plan distributions are paid (which results in more time for tax-deferred growth) by selecting the right beneficiaries for a retirement accounts. It is a good idea to consult with a specialist who can assist in selecting the proper people to designate as the primary and secondary beneficiaries. A specialist can also help one to understand how the distribution amounts are calculated***Weigh the tax effects of withdrawing retirement funds early.*** Large retirement account balances remaining in an individual's name at death may be subject to both estate taxes and income taxes, which could significantly reduce the balance remaining for the heirs.

Use gift tax exclusions, including paying certain medical and educational expenses. Each year, a donor may give $10,000 ($20,000 if a spouse joins in the gift) per donee without paying federal gift tax. These amounts are indexed for inflation. In addition, a donor can pay certain medical and educational expenses of the donee without any gift tax liability. Using these exclusions from gift tax to the maximum extent annually continues to be a good estate planning strategy.***Use all or part of the exemption from generation-skipping tax.*** Each individual can transfer, either during life or upon death, $1 million ($2 million if the spouse joins in the gift) free of the 55 percent federal generation-skipping transfer (GST) tax. These amounts are indexed for inflation. If an individual wants to maximize the amount of wealth which is transferred to future generations, one should consider using this exemption (and possibly leveraging this exemption through the use of life insurance) as early as possible. With proper planning, millions of additional dollars can be made available for future generations. One may have to file gift tax returns to allocate part of the GST exemption, even if the gifts fall under the annual exclusion.***Withdraw IRA funds for sixty days.*** Rather than borrow short-term funds from a third party, consider using an IRA funds for up to sixty days. To avoid tax, one must follow proper procedures.

Make taxable gifts to pay less in taxes. Although the federal estate and gift tax rates are based on the same tax rate schedule, the computation of the tax liability is very different. The federal gift tax is computed using the net amount gifted to the donee, while the federal estate tax is computed using the gross amount. For example, assume a donor with a 50% federal estate and gift tax rate has $1.5 million. The donor could make a gift of $1 million (and pay $500,000 in federal gift tax). If the donor dies with the $1.5 million, only $750,000 would be available for heirs after paying the $750,000 federal estate tax

Avoid ancillary probate in another state. Real estate and tangible personal property owned by a deceased individual but located in another state are subject to probate proceedings in that state. To avoid having to have more than one probate, consider transferring any out-of-state property, such as real estate, into a revocable living trust or into joint tenancy.

Weigh the effectiveness of a defective grantor trust. This type of trust is effective for estate-planning purposes. It is only "defective" for income tax purposes, which means that the person establishing the trust will continue to pay the tax on the income earned by the trust. Although the value of the trust is increased by the amount of the tax paid, this payment is currently not treated as an additional taxable gift to the beneficiaries of the trust.

Maximize contributions to retirement plans. It is important to verify the contributing of the maximum amount possible to employer-sponsored retirement plans and to any plans that have been established for self-employment income.

Consider the use of trusts for charitable giving. Charitable remainder trusts and charitable lead trusts are split-interest accounts. In a remainder trust, the income interest is payable for a term of years (maximum of 20) or for life to a noncharitable beneficiary, with the remainder going to qualified charities at the end of the income term. In the year the trust is funded, the donor has an income tax charitable deduction equal to the present value of the charity's remainder interest. A charitable lead trust provides an income stream to qualified charities and the remainder passes to noncharitable beneficiaries chosen by the donor. Whether the donor receives a charitable deduction depends on how the trust is structured. Gift tax consequences must also be considered for both types of trusts.

Weigh ordinary income taxation on retirement-plan distributions against capital gain rates on other investments. In some cases, it may be more advantageous for individuals approaching retirement to invest in equities outside of their retirement accounts so they can obtain the favorable capital gains rate when they "cash in" their investment. Retirement plan distributions are generally taxed at ordinary income tax rates, which can be more than 39.6%.

Tax Strategies for The Self-Employed

If self-employed, consider employing a under-18 child. A child who is under age 18 and employed by his or her self-employed parent in an unincorporated business is not subject to FICA taxes, and the parent is not responsible for paying the employer's portion of FICA taxes. Additionally, the parent is allowed a tax deduction for the wages paid to the child, and the child's standard deduction will shelter the first $4,300 of wages from tax. In essence, the parent is able to shift $4,300 of his or her income to each child tax free.

Take advantage of section 179 expensing. If certain requirements are met, an individual could expense up to $19,000 in purchases of qualifying property placed in service during the year 1999, instead of depreciating the expenditures over a longer time period. Then in 2000, the limit rose to $20,000.

The Keough Defined Contribution plan have two variations: profit-sharing and money-purchase. The profit-sharing version of the Keogh is most like the SEP; because there is a ceiling on contributions - 25% of compensation, up to a maximum contribution of $49,000 in 2010 - and below that limit you can put in whatever you can spare. The contribution amount can also be changed each year. With the money-purchase plan, a percentage of income is chosen and the investor will contribute every year consistently or else the IRS will assign a penalty.

Establish a Keogh retirement plan before the last day of the year. If an individual is self-employed and wants to deduct contributions to a new Keogh retirement plan for the 2011 tax year, he or she must establish the plan by the last day of the year. One does not actually have to put the money into a Keogh(s) until the due date of a tax return.

Don't forget deductions for health insurance premiums. If self-employed (or are a partner or a 2% S corporation shareholder-employee), for the current year, one may deduct 60 % of personal medical insurance premiums as an adjustment to gross income. This percentage is scheduled to increase in future years. The adjustment does not reduce net earnings subject to self-employment taxes, and it cannot exceed the earned income from the business under which the plan was established. One may not deduct premiums paid during a calendar month in which one is eligible for employer-paid health benefits.

Avoiding Estimated Tax Penalties

Federal tax law requires the payment of income taxes throughout the year as one earns an income. This obligation may be met through withholding or quarterly estimated tax payments or both. If estimated taxes are overpaid, an individual is in effect making an interest-free loan to the government. The penalty for underpayment is calculated as interest on the underpaid balance until it is paid. The interest rate on underpayments are adjusted under a prescribed formula in response to changes in federal short-term interest rates.

Methods for Avoiding Estimated Tax Penalties

There are several ways to avoid estimated tax penalties. The basic rule is to pay the required amount by the end of the year through withholding and quarterly estimated payments. The required amount will be one of the following, depending on the individual taxpayer's situation:

✓ *90% of the current year's tax liability.*

✓ *100% of the prior year's tax liability (increases to 105% for taxpayers who have adjusted gross income in excess of $150,000).*

✓ *90% of the tax liability based on a quarterly annualization of current year-to-date income*

Penalties are based on the difference between the lowest amount required to be paid by each quarterly payment date and the amount actually paid by that date. If payments are based on one of the first two alternatives above, the annual required amount must be divided equally among the four quarters to determine the cumulative amount due at each quarterly payment date. In the case of annualized income, however, the amount due by each payment date is determined based on income to date. Thus, the annualization method may be the one to use if much of the income is accrued or received during the latter part of the year, because the annualization method allows for lower required payments in the early quarters

Payments made through withholding from a paycheck (or from a pension or other payments) are given special treatment. The IRS treats income tax that is withheld as having been paid equally throughout the year. This lets an individual make up for underpaid amounts retroactively, because amounts withheld late in the year may be used to increase the amounts deemed paid in earlier quarters.

State and Local Rules

Most of the state and local taxing districts have similar rules and penalties related to the prepayment of income taxes during the year. Since many states have prepayment rules that vary from the federal requirements listed above, an individual needs to become familiar with the rules for the states and localities in which he or she files returns and take the steps necessary to avoid underpayment interest and penalties. One must therefore judge the adequacy of the tax payments to authorities at all levels.

Other Taxes

When computing required estimated tax payments, it is important to consider the increasing number of "other taxes" that apply in addition to the regular income tax. Some, such as the self-employment tax and the alternative minimum tax, have existed for many years. Others, such as the employment taxes for domestic employees, are relatively new.

Timing Income

Income is generally taxable to individual taxpayers in the year in which it is received. In general, a taxpayer may defer payment of tax by deferring receipt of the income. However, one cannot defer taxation by merely delaying receipt of the income if the funds are available to him or her and the time of payment is subject to a unrestricted discretion. If one operates a business or collect rental income and report that income on the cash receipts and disbursements method, one has the opportunity to delay or accelerate the billing to customers or tenants and determine the timing of the related income.

Timing Deductions

Opportunities for reducing taxable income may be available by controlling the payment of deductible expenses. One may deduct certain expenses that are due for payment next year on a return if they are paid by December 31. This strategy helps the most when one expects the marginal tax rate to be higher in the current year than in the next, because the rate differential makes the deduction worth more in the current year.

However, even if the tax rate is expected to be the same in the following year, it may still be worth paying some expenses a few months early in order to gain the tax benefit a full year sooner.

One can also pay a deductible expense in December, instead of April in the following year when it is due. Generally, this will be to the tax payer's advantage, unless he or she has an alternative use for the funds that will produce a very high return in that three- or four-month period.

Prepaid Interest

Although a cash-basis taxpayer generally may deduct expenses only in the year they are actually paid, there is an exception for prepaid interest expense.

Medical Expenses

If the timing of certain medical and dental expenditures is flexible and if overall medical expenses are high in the current year, one may want to accelerate payment of these expenses.

Miscellaneous Itemized Deductions

Miscellaneous itemized deductions are a defined group of deductions that one can deduct only to the extent that they exceed 2% of adjusted gross income.

Tax Credits

Tax credits provide another means to reduce overall tax liability.

Tax Tips for Business Owners

Consider establishing an employee stock ownership plan (ESOP) ~~ If an individual owns a business and needs to diversify a investment portfolio, it might be wise to consider establishing an ESOP. A properly funded ESOP provides a mechanism for selling shares with no current tax liability.

Make a succession plan ~~ Has a succession plan for both management and ownership of a business been planned for in the event of the owner's death or incapacity? Many business owners wait too long to recognize all the benefits from making a succession plan. These benefits include ensuring an orderly transition and ensuring the lowest possible tax cost. Waiting too long can be expensive from a financial perspective (covering gift and income taxes, life insurance premiums, appraiser fees, and legal and accounting fees) and from a nonfinancial perspective (intrafamily and intracompany squabbles).***Avoid nondeductible compensation*** ~~ Compensation can be deducted only if it is reasonable. Recent court decisions have allowed business owners to deduct compensation when (1) the corporation's success was due to the shareholder–employee, (2) the bonus policy was consistent, and (3) the corporation did not provide unusual corporate perquisites and fringe benefits.***Purchase Corporate Owned Life Insurance (COLI)*** ~~ COLI can be a tax-effective tool for funding deferred executive compensation, funding company redemption of stock as part of a succession plan, and providing many employees with life insurance in a highly leveraged program.

Avoid dividend treatment when a corporation purchases stock from family members ~~ In certain circumstances, the family member may be treated as receiving a dividend and have to pay tax at ordinary income rates on the entire amount of the redemption proceeds. If certain tests are met, the family member may instead report only capital gain equal to the difference between the proceeds and basis and pay tax at a maximum rate of 20%.

Consider establishing a SIMPLE retirement plan ~~ If an individual has no more than 100 employees and no other qualified plan, he or she may set up a Savings Incentive Match Plan for Employees (SIMPLE) into which an employee may contribute up to $11,500 in

2011. The employer, is required to make matching contributions. Talk with a benefits specialist to fully understand the rules and advantages and disadvantages of these accounts.

Guide to Reducing Taxes

The very word "Taxes" strikes fear into our hearts. In no uncertain terms, taxes are the means by which Uncle Sam confiscates money for his own use. And taxes come in many different forms. Income, sales, excise, gift, estate, luxury, and property and the list of different taxes goes on and on.

To build a sizable nest-egg for the family, one needs to do two things:

Maximize the money earned.

Minimize the money paid in taxes every year.

To effectively reduce taxes each year, one needs a set plan in place. Many choose to work with outside tax specialists who know the tax code inside and out. Others do their own research, managing their investments, doing their own tax returns, and ensuring that when April 15th rolls around, they're ready. No matter how one copes with his or her own tax problem, there are things that will dramatically reduce the taxes that are being paying.

For instance, the Taxpayer Relief Act of 1997 created hundreds of new tax breaks that can reduce an annual tax bill. Plus, the Act also increased the Unified Credit, currently set at $675,000.

Financial Planning for Long-Term Taxes

One will want to identify and quantify individual goals when looking at tax and financial situation from a long-term perspective. For example, one may want to retire at age sixty-five and be able to spend $50,000 per year after taxes. If an individual is currently age sixty-four, he or she does not have a long time in that to implement a plan. An individual can evaluate whether this goal is possible based on current assets and projected retirement income and make some adjustments as a result. If an individual is currently age 44, he or she can have a substantial effect on the ability to make a goal a reality.

On the other hand, one may not expect to retire in the conventional sense. It might still be nice to know when financial independence is achieved. By developing one's own individual definition of financial independence, he or she can evaluate whether it has been achieved—and still continue to work. The rest of this book will focus primarily on identifying the tax issues involved in long-term planning and giving one some perspective on the long-term issues.

Let us take for example a situation where an individual is offered a new job in another city with a moderate increase in pay. Is it wise for this individual to take the job? Many people hate to make decisions in their lives because they do not like the discomfort that comes with uncertainty and change. Still others proudly think of themselves as decision makers, relying on "gut feelings" to make choices. Both of these approaches might work at times, but each can be quite costly. There is a better way.

Estate Taxes

Many estate planning techniques have developed in response to a single fact: The federal and state governments may impose a tax when property is transferred to someone else after the owner dies. The federal estate tax is imposed on most types of property that a person transfers at death. Many examples of property are obvious: stocks, cash, and real estate. However, the tax can also be imposed in situations in which the deceased does not own the property but can direct where it passes.

Determining all of the elements that make up an individual's gross estate for tax purposes is beyond the scope of this general discussion. Instead, one should consider the following major points as he or she begins to develop a strategy for minimizing or reducing estate tax exposure.

Estate Tax Liability

The estate tax is progressive, so as the value of an estate increases, planning becomes more important. The marginal estate tax rate on a transfer of $10,000 is 18%, while the rate on a transfer in excess of $3,000,000 is 55%. The amount of tax computed is increased by 5% for taxable estates between $10 million and $17,184,000. This 5% surcharge eliminates the benefit of the graduated tax rates, resulting in an effective tax rate of 55% (60% in the phase-out range). Prior to the Taxpayer Relief Act of 1997, the 5% surcharge applied to taxable estates between $10 million and $24.1 million. The higher threshold eliminated the benefit of the unified credit. Congress may reinstate the unified credit surcharge in the future.

The estate tax is really a transfer tax because it applies to property transfers during lifetime (such as gifts) and at death (such as inheritances). As a result, an effective estate plan should consider both lifetime giving as well as the transfer of property at death. All such transfers may be subject to tax. More importantly, lifetime planning can significantly reduce any transfer tax liability at death.

Some types of transfers are excluded in determining the amount of a transfer that is subject to tax.

For simplicity, the remainder of the examples in this publication will assume the applicable exemption amount is $1 million. Estate administration expenses and debts can be deducted before computing any estate tax liability.

For a married couple, the primary deduction that reduces any gift or estate transfer tax is the marital deduction. This deduction is unlimited and permits one spouse to transfer any or all property to the other spouse free of tax. Thus, with proper planning, the estate transfer tax for married individuals can be deferred until the death of the surviving spouse. Amounts given to charity during lifetime or at death generally are not subject to any transfer tax.

After all exclusions and deductions have been considered, a tentative tax is computed on the remaining amount of transferred property. This tax can be offset by the applicable credit amount based upon the applicable exemption amount previously discussed. Thus, any estate with a total value less than the exemption amount will generally not be subject to any federal estate taxes.

Although the marital deduction allows for an unlimited amount of property to pass between spouses without transfer tax consequences, this deduction does not eliminate the need to develop an estate plan for the overall family. A simple estate plan under which everything passes to the surviving spouse may eliminate any taxes in the estate of the first to die; however, additional taxes may be due at the death of the surviving spouse. The marital deduction should be coordinated with each spouse's unified credit.

State death or inheritance taxes may have to be paid in addition to federal transfer taxes. Many state transfer taxes are patterned after the federal tax; however, there are differences, and state taxes may be incurred even in situations in which there is no federal tax.

Glossary

Adequate Protection—The standard of protection granted a creditor by the trustee or debtor-in-possession to avoid court sanctioned foreclosure on its property.

Administrator—The person appointed by the court to manage an estate when he or she dies without leaving a will. Since they are court appointed, they are required to post a bond as security. They have the same duties as an executor.

Amendment—This refers to a revision or addition to a trust document which either corrects an error, or changes the terms of the trust to coincide with the trustor's wishes.

Annual Exclusion—An exclusion from gift taxes for gifts by each donor to each donee, which is available on an annual basis. The annual exclusion is currently $10,000 per donee (and is indexed for inflation), per calendar year. That is, a couple with three children could give $60,000 per year tax free to the next generation. In order to qualify for the annual exclusion, the gift must be a "present interest" i.e., a gift available immediately to the donee as opposed to one not available until the future or one requiring the consent of some other person.

Applicable Credit Amount—An estate tax credit based upon the applicable exemption amount used to reduce the tax on transfers of property either during life (gift tax) or at death (estate tax). Created by the Taxpayer Relief Act of 1997, the applicable credit amount is $1,730,800 for 2011 and 2012.

Applicable Exemption Amount—For deaths occurring in 2011, up to $5,000,000 can be passed from an individual (for married couples, the applicable amount is $10,000,000) upon his or her death without incurring estate tax.

Attorney-in-fact—This refers to the individual who is designated in the power of attorney document to act on behalf of another.

Automatic Stay—An injunction, or court order, that takes effect when a bankruptcy petition is filed. An automatic stay prohibits all collection against a debtor.

Asset—The property of a testator or grantor, whether real or personal, which passes under a will and/or is placed into a trust account.

Asset Allocation—Investment assets can be placed into different categories for classification purposes. When an Investment Advisor assigns a percentage of the account investments to each of these categories, he is completing an Asset Allocation. Asset Allocation is an acceptable way for a manager or trustee to diversify risk and increase return in an investment portfolio.

Assignment—This is a document that assigns the interest of one party to another. When a grantor wants to place a contract or lease into a trust, an assignment of the grantor's interest is prepared to transfer the interest to the trust. The Assignor is the one conveying the interest and the Assignee is the one receiving the interest.

Avoidance Powers—The powers used by a trustee to reverse transfers of the debtor's property.

Balance Sheet—This refers to a statement of financial conditions as of a specific date. It is different from a cash flow statement, which summarizes income and expenses.

Bankruptcy Code—The legal instrument filed with the bankruptcy court that commences a bankruptcy proceeding.

Bankruptcy Petition—The legal instrument filed with the bankruptcy court that commences a bankruptcy proceeding.

Bar Date—This is the last date for filing a proof of claim.

Beneficiary—This refers to someone who receives benefits or funds under a will or other contract, such as an insurance policy.

Beneficiary Transfer—When one names a beneficiary in an insurance policy or in an employee benefit plan and the proceeds pay out to the beneficiary, the result is a beneficiary transfer.

Bequest—This means to leave (bequeath) personal property to another by Last Will and Testament.

Bypass Trust—A trust which contains property on which Federal Taxes are paid at the death of the first spouse to die, and which typically is not taxed at the second death. Where the optimum marital deduction plan is used, the tax on the property in this trust is paid by the Applicable Credit Amount and it is sometimes referred to as the Credit Shelter Trust.

Call Risk—This refers to the possibility that falling interest rates will cause a bond issuer to redeem—or call—its high-yielding bond before the bond's maturity date.

Chapter 7—In a Chapter 7 proceeding, the debtor's business is liquidated, and its assets are distributed to creditors with allowed proofs of claim.

Chapter 11—Normally, a Chapter 11 proceeding is a reorganization proceeding. The debtor continues to operate its business after the bankruptcy is filed. Chapter 11 liquidators are not uncommon and usually are the result of an unsuccessful reorganization attempt.

Closing—When a bankruptcy case is closed, it is no longer in the court's docket.

Codicil—To make an addition to a will, or to change, explain, revoke, or add provisions.

Co-Trustee—Whenever there are two or more concurrent trustees of a trust, they are called Co-Trustees.

Collateral—This refers to the property of a debtor in which a creditor has a lien securing its debt.

Community Property—Ten states (Alaska, Arizona, California, Idaho, Louisiana, Nevada, New Mexico, Texas, Washington, and Wisconsin) use some form of the community property system to determine the interest of a husband and wife in property acquired during marriage.

Complaint—A pleading that is filed to initiate a lawsuit or an adversary proceeding.

Composition—Out of court agreement to pay a percentage of a debt in full settlement.

Conversion—The conversion of a bankruptcy case from one chapter type to another.

Corporate Trustee—If an individual is the trustee of his or her own trust that individual is an individual trustee. When a bank, or trust company is named as the trustee it is known as a Corporate Trustee.

Country Risk—The possibility that political events (a war, national elections), financial problems (rising inflation, government default), or natural disasters (an earthquake, a poor harvest) will weaken a country's economy and cause investments in that country to decline.

Credit Risk—This refers to the possibility that a bond issuer will fail to repay interest and principal in a timely manner. Also called default risk.

Credit Shelter Trust— The Credit Shelter Trust allows each spouse to pass on an estate worth up to $2,000,000.00 without incurring any transfer taxes. This is called the "applicable exclusion amount." However, beginning in 2011, that amount drops to $1,000,000.

Crummey Trust—An irrevocable life insurance trust that has "Crummey Powers" incorporated into the document. The "Crummey Power" allows one to make a gift of up to $10,000 per donee, per year, (although usually less than this amount) into the trust. The current income beneficiary(s) has the right to withdraw the gifted amount during a specified period. If the withdrawal does not take place, the gift amount defaults to the trust, and remains in the trust to pay insurance premiums.

Currency Risk—The possibility that returns could be reduced for Americans investing in foreign securities because of a rise in the value of the U.S. dollar against foreign currencies.

Debtor—One who owes debts. In bankruptcy, the bankrupt business that is under the control and protection of the bankruptcy court is the debtor.

Debtor-In Possession (DIP)—The business debtor in a Chapter 11 reorganization. In a Chapter 11, the debtor retaining possession of the assets involved in the bankruptcy.

Decedent—The person who has died.

Devise—To leave property by will. Historically a "devise" only referred to a transfer of real property, not personal property, but Utah law now uses the term for both forms of property.

Discharge—A discharge in bankruptcy relieves the debtor of the dischargeable debts incurred prior to filing. Discharge is the legal term for the elimination of debt through bankruptcy.

Dismissal—The dismissal of a bankruptcy case, for all intents and purposes, returns the debtor to the same place it was before bankruptcy was filed.

DOD—A common abbreviation for "Date of Death."

Durable Power of Attorney—A written legal document that lets an individual designate another person to act on his or her behalf, even in the event the individual becomes disabled or incapacitated.

Durable Power of Attorney for Health Care—A written legal document that gives another person the authority to act on one's behalf regarding health care decisions.

Elective Share—The Elective Share is the share of a Decedent's assets which the surviving spouse can elect to receive, under the State probate code regardless of the provisions of the Decedent's Will or Trust. This share was formerly known as the "Dower" right and was equal to the amount the spouse would have received under the intestate succession statute if there had been no Will. The modern Elective Share was instituted under the Uniform Probate Code, which has been adopted by many states in the United States

Estate—The property or assets that an individual owns or has rights to.

Estate Plan—The overall plan devised by the estate planning professional with the help of the grantor, to pass the estate of the grantor on to the remainder beneficiaries. This plan usually includes wills, trusts, right to die documents, limited partnerships, limited liability companies, and related documents as drafted by the attorney. There may also be provisions on how to manage the assets of the grantors while they are still alive and capable, or if they should become incapacitated.

Estate Tax—A tax imposed at one's death on the transfer of most types of property.

Examiner—An officer of the court is sometimes appointed to investigate the financial affairs of the debtor.

Executor—The person named in a will to manage an estate. This person will collect the property, pay any debt, and distribute the property or assets according to the will.

Exemption or Exempt Property—Property of an individual debtor that the law protects from the actions of creditors, such as the debtor's residence or homestead, automobile, and the like.

Fiduciary—A person or institution legally responsible for the management, investment, and distributions of funds

Foreclosure—A debt-collection whereby property of the debtor is sold on the courthouse steps to satisfy debts. Foreclosure often involves real estate of the debtor.

Funding—The act of transferring the title to assets into the name of the trustee from the name of the grantor.

Generation Skipping Tax—This tax, instituted in 1984, taxes the transfer of wealth from the decedent to generations more remote than his or her children. Each person has an exemption of $1,030,000 from this tax(as indexed for inflation.) Once more that this amount has been left to a grandchild or great-grandchild, etc., a tax is imposed on the transfer at a flat 55% rate. The advent of this tax has curtailed the use of the "Generation Skipping Trust", so that such trusts now are usually the recipient of only the exempt amount, to be held for the benefit of remote beneficiaries.

Gift—A gratuitous transfer of property to someone else, without receiving adequate consideration in return.

Gift Program—Usually a planned program of making annual gifts to beneficiaries within the amount of the Annual Exclusion.

Grantor—The person who transfers assets into a trust for the benefit of another.

Gross Estate—The total property or assets held by an individual as defined for federal estate tax purposes.

Gross-up Gift taxes—If gifts have been made within three years of the year of death on which gift taxes were actually paid, those gift taxes will be added back to the value of the estate for purposes of computing the estate tax. This is called gift tax gross-up.

Guardian—The person legally entrusted with the care of a minor child.

Heir—A person who is to receive assets under the laws of intestacy in the absence of a will. In common usage, however, the term is inaccurately applied to a person who receives benefits as a beneficiary under the terms of a will.

Incapacity—The lack of ability to act on one's own behalf.

Income—Normally, the trust or will designates what income is and what is principal. In the absence of designation language, there is a "Uniform Principal and Income Act" under the "Uniform Probate Code" which would outline what is income and what is principal. If one lives in a" Non-Uniform Probate Code" state, then state statute will govern what to designate as income and principal in the absence of governing language in the document.

Income Beneficiary—The person who will receive the income from a trust for a specified period of time (e.g., "beneficiary for life").

Income Risk—The possibility that the dividends paid by a fixed-income investment, such as a bond, will decline because of falling overall interest rates.

Industry Risk—The possibility that a group of stocks in a single industry will decline in price due to developments in that industry.

Inflation Risk—The possibility that increases in the cost of living will reduce or eliminate an investment's real (inflation-adjusted) returns.

Inheritance Tax—Technically, a death tax which is levied by a State upon each taker of a decedents' property, as opposed to an estate tax which is levied on the estate as a whole.

Interest Rate Risk—The possibility that a bond investment will decline in value because of an increase in interest rates.

Inter vivos—A type of trust created during one's lifetime to hold property for the benefit of another.

Intestacy, Intestate—The term applied when an individual dies without a will.

Irrevocable—Indicating something that cannot be changed or terminated.

Joint Property – This is property where title is held in Joint Tenancy so that the surviving co-owner[s] own the entire asset by operation of law at the death of any owner. In a marriage, this property usually qualifies as marital property for marital deduction purposes

Joint Tenancy with Right of Survivorship—A title that can be placed on property that is co-owned. At the death of one of the co-owners, the other will become the sole owner of the property, regardless of what may be conveyed in the will.

Lien—An interest in property securing the repayment of a debt.

Life Insurance Gift Value—The value of a life insurance policy which is given to someone else. Normally, this value is very close to the cash surrender value. In most cases the gift value will be less than the face value of the policy. Where the insured is in bad health, and could not obtain new insurance within normal cost limits, the gift value of the policy may be greater that the face value.

Living Trust—A revocable trust established by a grantor during his or her lifetime in which the grantor transfers some or all of his or her property into the trust.

Living Will—A legal document directing that the maker's or signer's life is not to be artificially supported in the event of a terminal illness or accident.

Lump Sum Gift—Typically, a gift which is made on a one-time basis only, as opposed to a gift program, which is designed to use the annual exclusion on a yearly basis.

Manager Risk—The possibility that an actively managed stock or bond fund's investment adviser will fail to execute the fund's investment strategy effectively and, as a result, the fund will fail to achieve its stated objective.

Marital Deduction—A deduction allowing for the unlimited transfer of any or all property from one spouse to the other generally free of estate and gift tax.

Marital Property—In general usage, property acquired by a married couple during the marriage from their separate or joint efforts including wages, profits, etc. Marital Property is similar to what would be community property if the couple had resided in a community property state. Marital Property does not include gifts, inheritances or assets acquired prior to marriage.

Minor Child—A minor child is a person who has not yet reached the legal age of majority. This age can differ with each state, but generally is between 16 and 18 years. The term does not apply to an emancipated youth.

Marginal Estate Tax Rate—The tax rate at which the top dollars in an estate are taxed.

Market Risk—The possibility that stock or bond prices overall will decline over short or even extended periods. Stock and bond markets tend to move in cycles, with periods when prices rise and other periods when prices fall.

Motion—A request for the court to act. A motion may be filed within a lawsuit, adversary proceeding, or bankruptcy case.

Per Stirpes—A term used in a will or trust which designates that property will pass to descendants "by branches" so that a Decedent's children divide equally the same share the Decedent would have taken at each level of descent.

Personal Property—Property that is not permanently attached to land.

Personal Representative—The person who manages the assets of an estate, using the will, if any, as a guide, through the probate process. This person was formerly known as the Executor or Executrix.

Petition for Relief—The papers filed initiating a bankruptcy case.

Possessory Security Interest—A security interest or lien on property that requires the creditor to have possession of the property, such as a pawn or pledge.

Power of Appointment—A right given to another in a written instrument, such as a will or trust, that allows the other to decide how to distribute property. The power of appointment is "general" if it places no restrictions on who the distributees may be. A power is "limited" or "special" if it limits the eventual distributee.

Power of Attorney—Power of Attorney is a written legal document that gives an individual the authority to act for another.

Preference—A transfer of property of the debtor to a creditor made immediately prior to the debtor's bankruptcy that enables the creditor to receive more than it would have received from the bankruptcy. A preferential transfer must be made while the debtor was insolvent and as payment for a debt that existed prior to the transfer of property.

Principal Risk—The possibility that an investment will go down in value, or "lose money."

Probate—The review or testing of a will before a court of law to ensure that it is authentic.

Representative—Someone who is authorized to act on one's behalf, such as an executor or a trustee.

State Death or Inheritance Taxes—The tax imposed by the state in which an individual lives and/or where the property is located, if different, on the transfer of that property to another at one's death.

Successor Trustee—The person designated in the document or named later who assumes the duties of trustee after the death, incapacity, or resignation of the original trustee.

Survivor—Usually referring to the surviving spouse in a marriage.

Testamentary Trust—A trust that is created upon an individual's death by the terms of the will.

Testator/Testatrix—A person who makes a will.

Trust—A written legal instrument created by a grantor during his or her lifetime or at death for the benefit of another.

Trustee—This is the person named in a trust document who will manage the property owned by the trust and distribute any income according to the document. A trustee can be an individual or a corporate fiduciary.

Will—A formal testamentary document which outlines the wishes of the Testator or maker of the will. This document will normally outline who the beneficiaries are, and what assets are to be distributed to them. It will also name a "Personal Representative" (formerly known as an Executor) to manage the assets through the probate process.

Witness—A term used to describe those who attest to the validity of a will or trust. A will must be witnessed to be valid in most states. Witnesses should not have a beneficial interest in the will, and should be of sound mind and legal age

Page

Don't miss out!

Visit the website below and you can sign up to receive emails whenever Sharon O'Maley publishes a new book. There's no charge and no obligation.

https://books2read.com/r/B-A-NVXZ-XCWNC

BOOKS 2 READ

Connecting independent readers to independent writers.

About the Author

Sharon Finch O'Maley was born in Xenia, Ohio to a preacher and his wife, Ralph and Ruth Finch. She moved with her parents and older sister, Marilyn, to Indiana, New Jersey, Colorado, and back to Ohio and to Nebraska through her childhood. She graduated from college with a degree in Elementary Education. She taught school for the following seven years.

Her dream of being a missionary in a Spanish-speaking country came true in 1982 when she went to Costa Rica for five months. In 1986, she was assigned to go to the Dominican Republic for three years. Many of the stories in "At the Break Of Dawn" are her experiences with the people she loved so much.

Sharon is presently living in Austin, Texas and is the mother of a daughter, Ruth who attended University of Texas in Austin, Texas and is now married to her high school sweetheart, Steve Largaespada and has two young sons.

Sharon has been published in various magazines, newspapers, and daily devotional books. She is a daily blogger on Dr. Strains CBD.

www.ingramcontent.com/pod-product-compliance
Lightning Source LLC
LaVergne TN
LVHW022312200926
848481LV00004B/1310
* 9 7 9 8 2 2 3 5 6 4 2 7 0 *